Coping
with
Change
workbook

Facilitator Reproducible Guided Self-Exploration Activities

Ester R.A. Leutenberg
& John J. Liptak, Ed.D.

Illustrated by Amy L. Brodsky, LISW-S

WholePerson
Mental Health & Wellness
publisher of therapy, counseling, and self-help resources

Whole Person Associates

101 W. 2ⁿᵈ St., Suite 203
Duluth, MN 55802

800-247-6789

Books@WholePerson.com
WholePerson.com

Coping with Change Workbook
Facilitator Reproducible Guided Self-Exploration Activities

Printed in the United States of America

Editorial Director: Carlene Sippola
Art Director: Joy Morgan Dey

Library of Congress Control Number: 2011927805
ISBN: 978-1-57025-257-0

Using This Book

In today's society, many people find themselves living through multiple extensive and often debilitating changes in their lives. Your clients are among the people affected by these changes. Change manifests itself in many facets of a person's life.

- **Workplace** – Because the work world is changing, people find themselves experiencing a variety of changes: corporations outsourcing jobs to other parts of the world or they are being eliminated to save corporations money; robots are replacing human employees; retirement savings are diminishing or disappearing due to the downturns in the economy; and competition has increased for newly created jobs.

- **Health** – As society changes and people finding themselves trying to keep up, they experience more stress and anxiety. This increase in anxiety and stress then leads to more physical illnesses, psychological problems, changes in eating habits, increased injuries, and sleeping issues.

- **Home & Family** – Ways people experience a sense of home and family have changed dramatically in recent years. Some of these changes include fragmentation of families through divorce and separation or extended absences of one or both parents who must fulfill military responsibilities; single-parent households or decisions to send children to grandparents or other relatives; changing traditions in family celebrations or the absence of family traditions; and time constraints preventing meaningful family interactions.

- **Personal** – Changes in people's personal and social lives may be some of the biggest changes people experience. Some of these changes include financial struggles due to overspending and major debt, job loss, cultural differences, changes in residence, and the struggle to keep up with changes in technology.

Because of constant changes in daily life, people face perpetually increasing levels of stress. Although change has always been a part of the lives of human beings, the present rate of changes is increasing exponentially. It is the *speed* of change that increases the stress in peoples' lives. Change is not going to stop, and therefore, people must develop skills to manage stress carefully. Coping with change is rapidly becoming a critical life skill that can be the difference between living a life of success or one of disappointment.

Everyone adapts to change differently. The important tactic for each individual is to master the basic skills that are critical to move through change easily and effectively.

This book provides assessments and self-guided activities to help people learn effective skills for coping with all forms of change. A variety of self-exploration activities are provided for you to determine which best suit the unique needs of your participants.

Information about Change

Moving through change can be difficult. The path through change is probably not going to be predictable or smooth for most people. Usually people navigate change and transition by moving through a series of five stages:

STAGE 1: SHOCK – People in this stage attempt to deny the news about a current or future change. They might say things like *"No, not me!"* or *"It can't be true!"* This stage is full of anxiety and runs its course in a relatively short time. It is considered a state of denial.

STAGE 2: ANGER – In this stage people begin to get angry. Initially they feel anger toward the people they feel are responsible for their change and blame others. After they have expressed their anger at outside sources, they may feel angry at themselves. Their anger is turned inward and becomes self-critical. They may say things like *"If only I . . ."* or *"If I would have . . . "*

STAGE 3: BARGAINING – People in this stage become calculating and reflective. Some attempt to make a deal with their higher power or the people involved in the change process. As their attempts to compromise fail, they usually give up and move to the next stage. They ask such questions as *"What can I do now?"* or *"Please give me another chance."* They try to identify their options and wish that things could be different.

STAGE 4: DEPRESSION – People in this stage begin to feel sad and/or depressed and think there are limited or no options. They often become silent and withdrawn. They begin to experience increasing weakness, discomfort and personal deterioration. They may feel a sense of meaninglessness, frustration, self-doubt, and lethargy, and they may want to be left alone. They may feel guilty and unworthy and feel as if nobody cares what happens to them.

STAGE 5: ACCEPTANCE – People in this stage are at the end of their struggle. They accept that change happens to everyone, that changes can be overcome, and that a change may even be an opportunity. They focus on the realities of the situation and begin to let go of their negative feelings. They notice that the pain begins to lessen and the struggle seems less difficult. They recognize that it is time to move on with their lives. They accept their *new normal.*

How Change Affects People

For the Facilitator and the Participant

Facts about change:

1. Change is a part of life. It is important to be able to cope with and manage change effectively.

2. All people go through a cycle of thoughts and emotions of some degree when they encounter change in their life. They need to keep in mind that these thoughts and emotions will not last. It is necessary to go through the stages in order to cope effectively with the change. The assessments, activities and exercises contained in this workbook will help people to move through the stages to acceptance more quickly.

3. Change can be managed. By completing the activities and exercises included in this workbook, participants will be able to not only cope with change, but to use change as opportunities for welcome and exciting transformations.

4. It is important for people to take control over changes in their life by taking responsibility for how they respond to the changes. They learn that they have the power to control what they think, feel and do. They recognize that they can care for themselves and relate effectively with others close to them.

Responding to Change:

Change produces unique signals that people can learn to read so they can respond to them sooner. The sooner they are able to take action to cope with their change and ultimate transition, the more likely they are to be effective in the change management process. When they find themselves going through a change, they will be alert to the signals produced by body, mind and emotion.

Emotions – People need to be aware when they are experiencing changes in their moods and feelings. Some of these changes might include feelings of anger, increased anxiety, moodiness, frustration, depression and withdrawal. Their behaviors may also include lashing out at others.

Mind – People need to be aware when they begin to have excessive negative thoughts that cause confusion, distraction, difficulty in concentrating at home and at work, a decrease in productivity, an increase in forgetfulness, and difficulty "turning their mind off" at night to sleep.

Body – People need to be aware of their body's negative reactions to the change process including such symptoms as an increase in headaches, colds, and flu symptoms, digestion problems, minor aches and pains, major illnesses, feelings of exhaustions, and muscle aches and pains.

Format of Book

The *Coping with Change Workbook* contains assessments and guided self-exploration activities that can be used with a variety of populations to help participants cope more effectively with the various forms of anxiety. Each chapter of this workbook begins with an annotated Table of Contents with notes and examples for the facilitator. Each chapter contains two primary elements: 1) A set of assessments to help participants gather information about themselves in a focused situation, and 2) a set of guided self-exploration activities to help participants process information and learn more effective ways of behaving to cope with anxiety in their lives.

Assessments

Each chapter begins with an assessment that provides participants with valuable information about themselves. These assessments can enhance recognition of effective and ineffective patterns of behavior, identify life skills which are productive and unproductive, and enrich participants' understanding of how they interact with the world. Assessments provide a path to self-discovery through the participants' exploration of their own unique traits and behaviors. The purpose of these assessments is not to "pigeon-hole" people, but to allow them to explore various elements that are critical for coping with anxiety. This book contains *self-assessments* and not *tests*. Traditional tests measure knowledge or right or wrong responses. For the assessments provided in this book, remind participants that there are no right or wrong answers. These assessments ask only for opinions or attitudes about topics related to a variety of coping skills and abilities.

The assessments in this book are based on self-reported data. In other words, the accuracy and usefulness of the information is dependent on the information that participants honestly provide about themselves. All of the assessments in this workbook are designed to be administered, scored, and interpreted by the participants as a starting point for them to begin to learn more about themselves and their coping skills. Remind participants that the assessments are exploratory exercises and not a final determination of abilities. Lastly, the assessments are not a substitute for professional assistance. If you feel any of your participants need more assistance than you can provide, please refer them to an appropriate professional.

As your participants begin the assessments in this workbook give these instructions:

- Take your time. Because there is no time limit for completing the assessments, work at your own pace. Allow yourself time to reflect on your results and how they compare to what you already know about yourself.

- Do not answer the assessments as you think others would like you to answer them or how you think others see you. Remember that these assessments are for you to reflect on your life and explore some of the barriers that are keeping you from living a calmer, more rational and less anxious life.

Format of Book *(Continued)*

- Assessments are powerful tools if you are honest with yourself. Take your time and be truthful in your responses so that your results are an honest reflection of you. Your level of commitment in completing the assessments honestly will determine how much you learn about yourself.

- Before completing each assessment, be sure to read the instructions. The assessments have similar formats, but they have different scales, responses, scoring instructions and methods for interpretation.

- Finally, remember that learning about yourself should be a positive and motivating experience. Don't stress about taking the assessments or finding out about your results. Just respond honestly and learn as much about yourself as you can.

Guided Self-Exploration Activities

Guided self-exploration activities are any exercises that assist participants in self-reflection and enhance self-knowledge, identify potential ineffective behaviors, and teach more effective ways of coping. Guided self-exploration is designed to help participants make a series of discoveries that lead to increased social and emotional competencies, as well as to serve as an energizing way to help participants grow personally and professionally. They are brief, easy-to-use self-reflection tools designed to promote insight and self-growth. Many different types of guided self-exploration activities are provided for you to pick and chose the activities most needed by your participants and/or will be most appealing to them. The unique features of self-guided exploration activities make them usable and appropriate for a variety of individual sessions and group sessions.

Features of Guided Self-Exploration Activities

- **Quick, easy and rewarding to use** – These guided self-exploration activities are designed to be an efficient, appealing method for motivating participants to explore information about themselves - including their thoughts, feelings, and behaviors - in a relatively short period of time.

- **Reproducible** – Because the guided self-exploration activities can be reproduced by the facilitator, no more than the one book needs to be purchased. You may photocopy as many items as you wish for your participants. If you want to add or delete words on a page, make one photocopy, delete and/or write your own words, and then make photocopies from your personalized master.

- **Participative** – Guided self-exploration activities help people to focus their attention quickly, aid them in the self-reflection process, and define new and more effective ways of coping.

Format of Book *(Continued)*

- **Motivating to complete** – Guided self-exploration activities are designed to be an energizing way for participants to engage in self-reflection and learn about themselves. Various activities are included to enhance the learning process related to developing important social and emotional competency skills.

- **Low risk** – Guided self-exploration activities are designed to be less risky than formal assessments and structured exercises. They are user-friendly, and participants will generally feel rewarded and motivated after completing these activities.

- **Adaptable to a variety of populations** – The guided self-exploration activities can be used with many different populations, and they can be tailored to meet the needs of the specific population with whom you work.

- **Focused** – Each guided self-exploration activity is designed to focus on a single coping issue, thus deepening the experience for participants.

- **Flexible** – The guided self-exploration activities are flexible and can be used independently, or to supplement other types of interventions.

Chapter Elements

The *Coping with Change Workbook* is designed to be used either independently or as part of an integrated curriculum. You may administer any of the assessments and the guided self-exploration activities to an individual or a group with whom you are working, or you may administer any of the activities over one or more days. Feel free to pick and choose those assessments and activities that best fit the outcomes you desire.

The first page of each chapter begins with an annotated Table of Contents with notes and examples for the facilitator.

Assessments – Assessments with scoring directions and interpretation materials begin each chapter. The authors recommend that you begin presenting each topic by asking participants to complete the assessment. Facilitators can choose one or more, or all of the activities relevant to their participants' specific needs and concerns.

Guided Self-Exploration Activities – Practical questions and activities to prompt self-reflection and promote self-understanding are included after each of the assessments. These questions and activities foster introspection and promote pro-social behaviors and coping skills. The activities in this workbook are tied to the assessments so that you can identify and select activities quickly and easily.

The activities are divided into four chapters to help you identify and select assessments easily and quickly:

Chapter 1: Types of Change – This chapter helps participants identify and explore the changes that are currently occurring in their lives, as well as identify and explore the changes they anticipate in the future.

Chapter 2: Change Management – This chapter helps participants identify the life skills they possess in managing the changes in their lives.

Chapter 3: Ways to Cope with Change – This chapter helps participants to explore how well they are coping with change in their lives, and to learn some techniques for enhancing their ability to cope with change.

Chapter 4: My Attitude About Change – This chapter helps participants explore their attitudes related to future change in their lives.

Thanks to . . .

Amy Brodsky, LISW-S, illustrator extraordinaire,
and to the following professionals whose input in this book has been invaluable!

Carol Butler, MS Ed, RN, C   Kathy Liptak, Ed.D.

Kathy Khalsa, MAJS, OTR/L   Eileen Regen, M.Ed., CJE

Jay Leutenberg

Table of Contents

Types of Change Scale

Change Management Scale

Table of Contents *(continued)*

Ways to Cope with Change Scale

My Attitude About Change Scale

Types of Change

Table of Contents and Facilitator Notes

Review the stages of change with the group and then give each participant the handout to complete the questions at the end of the page. If they wish, they may share with the group.

For homework, ask participants if they can find other quotations about change to share with the group.

After completing the handout, ask participants if they can pantomime or act out some of the feelings they listed on the handout, and ask others to guess the feeling.

After the handouts are completed, ask if participants will share their "What Ifs."

An example to the participants might be, "My thoughts are wondering if I've made a mistake by taking the job and moving. My emotion is sadness, worry and guilt. I then cry and become irritable."

Explain to participants that drawings do not need to be intricate. If they feel joyful and happy gardening, drawing a rake would be perfect.

Inform participants that they can feel free to share their feelings on this page and then tear it up, save it, or share those feelings with people involved.

After participants have completed the page, ask if anyone would be willing to share the activities they are considering.

Table of Contents and Facilitator Notes

Types of Change Scale Introduction

People experience changes in their personal lives, at home or at work – in fact, in any aspect of life. A little bit of change can usually be managed. However, it is imperative to identify the aspects of your life in which you are experiencing a great deal of change, and find that the pace and/or severity of change may be overwhelming.

The *Types of Change Scale* contains descriptors of the types of change you may be experiencing, or have recently experienced. Place a check in each of the boxes that describe changes you have recently experienced or are currently experiencing. The example below shows that the person completing the assessment has experienced a change in supervisors recently and not a change in job or new job responsibilities.

The type of CHANGE I have experienced or am experiencing now:

WORK

❏ Job

☑ Supervisor

❏ Increase of new job responsibilities

This is not a test and there are no right or wrong answers. Do not spend too much time thinking about your answers. Your initial response will be the most true for you.
Be sure to respond to every statement.

Name _____ **Date** _____

Turn to the next page and begin.

Scale: Types of Change

The type of CHANGE I have experienced or am experiencing now:

WORK

- ❑ Job
- ❑ Supervisor
- ❑ Increase of job responsibilities
- ❑ Layoff or loss of job
- ❑ Reduction in salary
- ❑ New technology
- ❑ Required to upgrade skills
- ❑ Decrease in work responsibilities
- ❑ Lack of control
- ❑ Reorganization
- ❑ Retirement
- ❑ Co-worker difficulties
- ❑ Searching for a job
- ❑ Taking a new position
- ❑ Going back to school
- ❑ Other _____
- ❑ Other _____
- ❑ Other _____

☑ WORK TOTAL = _____

PERSONAL

- ❑ Illness
- ❑ Injury
- ❑ Mental, physical or learning disability
- ❑ Eating habits
- ❑ Belief system
- ❑ Social life
- ❑ Accident
- ❑ Diagnosis of illness
- ❑ Aging issues
- ❑ Relationship problems
- ❑ Loss
- ❑ Legal difficulties
- ❑ Involved with Armed Forces
- ❑ Alternative lifestyle
- ❑ Residence
- ❑ Other _____
- ❑ Other _____
- ❑ Other _____

☑ PERSONAL TOTAL = _____

(Continued on the next page)

Scale: Types of Change *(continued)*

The type of CHANGE I have experienced or am experiencing now:

RELATIONSHIPS

- ❏ Significant other
- ❏ Marriage
- ❏ Children issues
- ❏ Loss of friend
- ❏ Birth of a child
- ❏ Loss of pregnancy
- ❏ Break-up
- ❏ Adoption
- ❏ Blended family
- ❏ In-laws
- ❏ Health of a family member
- ❏ Care of aging parents
- ❏ Empty nest
- ❏ Grandchildren
- ❏ Loss of family member
- ❏ _____
- ❏ _____
- ❏ _____

☑ **RELATIONSHIPS TOTAL =** _____

FINANCIAL

- ❏ Debt
- ❏ Major purchase
- ❏ Unaffordable / costly move
- ❏ New mortgage
- ❏ Business loss
- ❏ Loss of retirement income
- ❏ Financial loss
- ❏ Sale of a home
- ❏ Decrease in salary
- ❏ Inability to retire
- ❏ Overspending
- ❏ Financial gain
- ❏ Victim of theft
- ❏ Property loss or damage
- ❏ Legal problems
- ❏ _____
- ❏ _____
- ❏ _____

☑ **FINANCIAL TOTAL =** _____

GO TO THE SCORING DIRECTIONS

Types of Change Scale
Scoring Directions

Because it is a normal aspect of everyone's life, everyone experiences change. It is important to identify the aspects of your life in which you are experiencing major changes. You need to become aware of them and notice how these changes affect you. This assessment will help you explore the various ways you are experiencing change in your life. For each of the sections, count the number of boxes in which you placed a check. You will receive a score from 0 to 38. Put that total on the line marked TOTAL at the end of each section.

Transfer your totals to the spaces below:

✓ _____ = WORK TOTAL

✓ _____ = PERSONAL TOTAL

✓ _____ = RELATIONSHIPS TOTAL

✓ _____ = FINANCIAL TOTAL

Profile Interpretation

Individual Scales Scores	Result	Indications
13 to 18	high	If you score high on any of the scales, you have experienced, or are presently experiencing, a great deal of change in that area of your life.
7 to 12	moderate	If you score moderate on any of the scales, you have experienced, or are presently experiencing, some change in that area of your life.
0 to 6	low	If you score low on any of the scales, you have not experienced, or are not presently experiencing, much change in that area of your life.

No matter how you scored, low, moderate or high, you will benefit from the exercises that follow.

Stages of Change

When you go through a change, you experience a variety of feelings as you pass through five basic life stages:

STAGE 1 – SHOCK: In this stage you may be confused about the changes that are occurring in your life. You may be denying the fact that things are really changing. You may be saying to yourself such things as *"How can this happen to me?"* You are probably shocked by the realization that things will be different. You are probably feeling inadequate, questioning your self-worth, and maybe even feeling guilty.

STAGE 2 – ANGER: In this stage you may be angry at people causing the change in your life, and you may be blaming them. After you have expressed your anger at all possible outside sources, you may feel angry at yourself. Your anger is turned inward. Second guessing then begins to become self-criticism. You may be saying to yourself such things as *"If I had only …"*

STAGE 3 – BARGAINING: In this stage you are calculating and reflective. You attempt to influence outside sources by bargaining for the change not to occur. As your attempts to compromise fail, you give up. You ask such questions as *"What can I do now?"* You try to identify your options. You are probably wishing that things could be different. Your mental focus is on the future and on the possibilities that are available. You feel like you have done everything that you could do. You feel that when you get through this ordeal, you will be a better person for it.

STAGE 4 – DEPRESSION: In this stage you feel depressed. Because you have focused so much on your situation, you have become silent and withdrawn. You may feel a sense of meaninglessness. You are probably frustrated and doubting yourself. You feel lethargic and simply want to be left alone. You may be depressed by your view of what has happened. You are probably saying to yourself, *"There is no way I can bounce back from this."* You may even feel as if nobody cares what happens to you.

STAGE 5: ACCEPTANCE – In this stage you realize that what has happened is in the past. You accept the fact that you can no longer go back to the way things were and that it is time to move forward with your life. You are focusing on the realities of your situation and experience more energy as you begin your new life. You have probably analyzed your possibilities and are generating a new "game" plan. You have adjusted and are excited about getting on with your life.

What change are you currently going through? _____

_____

What stage have you already experienced? _____

_____

What stage are you in now? _____

_____

"...Be Afraid of Standing Still"

"Be not afraid of changing slowly; be afraid of standing still."

~ Chinese Proverb

Think about the quote you just read. Answer the following questions.

What thoughts do you have about this quote?

_____

_____

_____

_____

_____

_____

How does it apply to your life?

_____

_____

_____

_____

_____

_____

How does it describe change in your life?

_____

_____

_____

_____

_____

_____

What Am I Feeling?

To move more rapidly through the Stages of Change it is important for you to begin focusing on and understanding your feelings.

Describe a change in your life right now.

_____

_____

Describe the emotion you are feeling the most.

_____

_____

How intense is that feeling? Place an X on the line to describe your feelings.

VERY INTENSE	SOMEWHAT INTENSE	A LITTLE INTENSE	NOT VERY
10	5		0

What do you think has prompted you to feel this way?

_____

_____

Is your perception accurate? Place an X on the line to describe the accuracy of your thoughts.

VERY INTENSE	SOMEWHAT INTENSE	A LITTLE INTENSE	NOT VERY
10	5		0

How do you know this?

_____

_____

What conclusion can you come to?

_____

_____

_____

The *WHAT IF* Game

When people are going through changes they often allow their imagination to run wild. They find themselves playing the *What If* game.

In the *What If* game, you keep trying to find the reason for the change and wondering if you could have done something differently to have avoided the change. In the *What If* box below, describe some of the *What Ifs* you said to yourself the last time you experienced a change in your life.

The Change _____

_____

What if _____

Would it have helped the situation? _____

_____

_____

Would it have made a difference? _____

_____

_____

Is this realistic thinking? _____

_____

_____

Monitor Your Self-Thoughts

In times of change, you probably have a constant dialog going on in your head. When you are in the midst of change, you have a stream of mostly negative thoughts that invade your thinking. These thoughts can then lead to negative emotions. List a situation regarding a change you experienced or are currently experiencing.

#1 THOUGHTS IN MY HEAD	#2 THOUGHTS IN MY HEAD	#3 THOUGHTS IN MY HEAD
_____ _____ _____ _____ ↓	_____ _____ _____ _____ ↓	_____ _____ _____ _____ ↓
EMOTIONS THESE THOUGHTS LEAD TO _____ _____ _____ _____ ↓	EMOTIONS THESE THOUGHTS LEAD TO _____ _____ _____ _____ ↓	EMOTIONS THESE THOUGHTS LEAD TO _____ _____ _____ _____ ↓
THE RESULT OF THESE NEGATIVE EMOTIONS _____ _____ _____ _____ ↓	THE RESULT OF THESE NEGATIVE EMOTIONS _____ _____ _____ _____ ↓	THE RESULT OF THESE NEGATIVE EMOTIONS _____ _____ _____ _____ ↓

How can you stop these thoughts?

_____

_____

_____

Joy

While going through changes, people often focus too much on the negatives in their lives and forget about the things they have to be grateful for the people and moments that bring joy into their lives.
Write and/or draw your responses.

What are the blessings in your life?	How do you express your gratitude?
What makes you most happy?	Who brings you happiness?
What changed and caused you to lose some of the joy in your life?	How can you enjoy your life more?

© 2011 WHOLE PERSON ASSOCIATES, 101 WEST 2ND ST., SUITE 203, DULUTH MN 55802 • 800-247-6789

Accepting Change
and Acknowledging Feelings

Write a letter about the change you are experiencing or have experienced. Describe how this change is affecting or has affected your life and the lives of those around you. Acknowledge the emotions you are feeling.

I, (name)_____, have a major change

that has occurred in my life. The change is _____

_____.

I have been feeling _____

_____

_____

_____ about the change. I am

working to feel better about myself and my situation. This change concerns me because

_____

_____.

It has affected me _____

_____.

It has also affected these people in my life _____

_____

_____.

They have been affected in these ways _____

_____

_____.

I am going to look at this change as an opportunity for _____

_____

_____

_____

_____.

Let Go of Your Feelings in a Healthy Way

When you are feeling stressed due to life changes, it is important
for you to learn a variety of ways to let go of your feelings in healthy ways.
Place a check (✓) by those you already use and
put a circle (◯) around those you will consider.

Art work	Knit	Crafts	Listen to music	Sing
Entertain at home	Express your feelings	Fly a kite and 'let it go'	Eat healthy	Get a medical check-up
Garden	Aerobics	Weight lift	Cook	Run
Become totally absorbed	Watch a comedy	Don't blame yourself	Create poetry	Positive Self-talk
Go out and have fun	Work on being positive	Dance	Remember, this too will pass	Reach out to supports
Martial Arts	Play sports	Swim	Organize	Avoid the blame game
Meditate	Watch sports	Jog	Walk	Count your blessings
See it from the future	Scream in a pillow	Go shopping	Run	Spend time in nature
Start a new hobby	Join a support group	Play with a baby or child	Confide in a trusted friend	Journal
Work out	Walk a dog	House project	Hike	Clean
Write a worse-case scenario	Volunteer at a food kitchen	Help out at a homeless shelter	Cry if you feel like it	Shift your focus
Yoga	Chop wood	Water exercise	Bake	Write a letter
Laugh	Have a good night's sleep	Eliminate caffeine	Volunteer in a local school	Yard work
Attend a play	Go to a concert	Stomp, kick or hit something	Have finances in order	Smile
Volunteer to read to patients	Write a short story	List possible actions	Sleep on it	Have lunch with a friend

Share Your Feelings

People going through changes often need to allow themselves to experience what they are feeling. These feelings may be positive feelings like peace, joy and relief. On the other hand, these feelings may be negative feelings like sadness, anger and loneliness.

What is a change that you are going through now or possibly in the future?

_____

_____

_____

_____

Write your feelings about this change. Enter all of your feelings, and draw a star next to your strongest feelings.

_____   _____   _____

_____   _____   _____

_____   _____   _____

What seems to be triggering these intense emotions?

_____

_____

_____

_____

Share your feelings with someone you care about. List some people you can trust, people with whom you feel comfortable and safe.

_____   _____

_____   _____

_____   _____

_____   _____

Getting Stuck in Your Feelings

When experiencing change, especially major change or multiple changes, it is easy to get stuck in negative feelings and have difficulty overcoming them. Following is a list of early warning signs to help you determine if you are getting stuck in negative emotions. For each warning sign, write about how it applies to you.

Losing interest in activities

_____

_____

Feeling ill frequently

_____

_____

Being tired a lot of the time

_____

_____

Losing desire to be with family and friends

_____

_____

Feeling down a lot of the time

_____

_____

Having troubled sleep or taking many naps

_____

_____

Avoiding tasks that you used to do easily

_____

_____

Being irritable

_____

_____

Arguing with others

_____

_____

Viewing the Future

Many people refuse to accept change in their lives because of the fear of what lies ahead in their lives. Think about the future.

My change . . .

_____

_____

_____

My fear about this change …

_____

_____

_____

To whom I can talk to about this fear?

_____

_____

_____

How I can overcome or cope with this fear?

_____

_____

_____

Types of Change

Moving from the Past

All change involves loss of some sort.

Write about a recent major change you have just been through.

_____

_____

What did you lose?

_____

_____

_____

_____

What has been negative about this change?

_____

_____

_____

_____

What has been positive about this change?

_____

_____

_____

_____

What is your "new normal" now?

_____

_____

_____

_____

Saying Good-Bye

**To put closure on your unfinished business,
it is important to say good-bye to your former situation
and express your feelings about it.**

Your changed situation _____

_____

_____

I would like to say good-bye	My feelings
_____	_____
_____	_____
_____	_____
_____	_____
_____	_____
_____	_____
_____	_____
_____	_____
_____	_____
_____	_____

Blaming

**Write about a major change you have experienced or
are currently experiencing.**

_____

_____

_____

Whom do you blame for your situation?

_____

_____

_____

_____

The reason is …

_____

_____

_____

_____

What do you accomplish by blaming this person?

_____

_____

_____

_____

How can you look at this differently?

_____

_____

_____

_____

Change Management

Table of Contents and Facilitator Notes

If participants are willing to share, ask them to describe their coping styles. They may want to form groups and talk about what they have in common and how their style works for them.

After participants have completed the handout, ask if people are willing to share what they learned about themselves.

Feel free to discuss any poem structure(s). As a warm-up exercise, the group can be divided into two, three or four partners, write poems and then share them with the group. This will prepare the participants to be able to write their own poems.

This activity is designed to help participants realize that often what they believe to be the worst that can happen is not always that bad at all.

These self-talk affirmations can be cut out and placed in strategic spots to remind participants to read them several times daily. There are three blank spots for participants to write their own. Brainstorm with group possibilities for the three blanks.

If participants are willing, it may be enjoyable to set up a debate. If there is no one who would be able to debate for the 'change is good' viewpoint, facilitator can take that position.

Table of Contents and Facilitator Notes

Bring a few examples of eye-catching headlines from the newspaper. Examples: "Planning Retirement – Scared", "Lost Job, Now What?" Remind participants they can use the reverse side of the page to continue writing.

An extra activity with this page might be to pick a change (moving to another city, losing a job, retiring) and ask everyone to complete the page with the same change. Then ask participants to discuss their responses.

Explain to the group that they can draw pictures in colors, use stick figures, cut pictures out of magazines, doodle, etc. Provide pencils, markers, crayons and magazines. Also have larger pieces of paper handy for them, if they wish to have more room to express themselves.

This activity promotes self-esteem and self-image. It can be completed individually with the participants and/or can be facilitated in a circle, with each person answering a question. Participants can pass if they prefer not to respond, and other people might want to interject their thoughts on others' questions, if time allows.

Have highlighters available in three colors, designating which color to use for each grouping.

Remind participants that doodling can be silly or serious drawings, abstract shapes or stick figures. No one needs to be able to interpret the drawing – they are doing it for themselves.

© 2011 WHOLE PERSON ASSOCIATES, 101 WEST 2ND ST., SUITE 203, DULUTH MN 55802 • 800-247-6789

Change Management Scale Introduction

Basic coping skills are detrimental in dealing effectively with a variety of changes. These changes take many forms in many different life roles and could include dealing with the loss of a loved one, loss of a job, or divorce. We are all able to cope differently with life transitions.

The *Change Management Scale* will help you identify your strengths in managing change. In addition, it will help you identify some skills that might help you cope effectively with your life changes.

In the following example, the circled numbers indicate how much the statement is descriptive of the person completing the scale.

3 = Very   2 = Somewhat   1 = Not at All

I. In dealing with transitions in your life, how effective have you been using these strategies:

1. developing a way to respond to change with a positive attitude . . . . . (3)   2   1
2. seeing problematic situations as a normal part of life 3   2   (1)

This is not a test and there are no right or wrong answers. Do not spend too much time thinking about your answers. Your initial response will be the most true for you.

Be sure to respond to every statement.

Name _____ Date _____

Turn to the next page and begin.

Scale: Change Management

3 = Very	2 = Somewhat	1 = Not at All

I. In dealing with transitions in your life, how effective have you been using these strategies:

1. developing a way to respond to change with a positive attitude 3   2   1

2. seeing problematic situations as a normal part of life 3   2   1

3. believing that you can cope with problematic situations effectively . . . 3   2   1

4. describing problematic situations effectively 3   2   1

5. not acting impulsively 3   2   1

6. resisting the tendency to do nothing 3   2   1

I - TOTAL = _____

II. In dealing with transitions in your life, how effective have you been using these strategies:

7. identifying and understanding your personal strengths 3   2   1

8. reaching out for support during the change 3   2   1

9. creating opportunities 3   2   1

10. changing negative thoughts into positive ones 3   2   1

11. viewing transitions as opportunities for growth 3   2   1

12. spending time with optimistic and supportive people 3   2   1

II- TOTAL = _____

(Continued on the next page)

Scale: Change Management

3 = Very   2 = Somewhat   1 = Not at All

III. In dealing with transitions in your life, how effective have you been using these strategies:

13. practicing techniques to relax yourself 3   2   1

14. expressing your emotional needs during transition periods 3   2   1

15. not allowing yourself to get too excited or depressed 3   2   1

16. taking care of yourself 3   2   1

17. recognizing pessimistic feelings 3   2   1

18. identifying the best way of responding to change 3   2   1

III - TOTAL = _____

IV. In dealing with transitions in your life, how effective have you been using these strategies:

19. knowing how you would like your life to be 3   2   1

20. developing a plan for new options and opportunities 3   2   1

21. identifying new goals to work toward 3   2   1

22. implementing and executing the chosen courses of action 3   2   1

23. identifying obstacles to achieving your goals 3   2   1

24. remaining committed to your goals 3   2   1

IV - TOTAL = _____

GO TO THE SCORING DIRECTIONS

Change Management Scale
Scoring Directions

The *Change Management Scale* is designed to measure the strength of your ability to cope with changes in your life. For each of the sections, count the scores you circled for each of the four sections. Put that total on the line marked TOTAL at the end of each section.

Then, transfer your totals to the spaces below:

TOTALS

I. _____ = Perceiving and Responding to Transitions

II. _____ = Developing and Utilizing Internal / External Support Systems

III. _____ = Reducing Emotional and Physical Distress

IV. _____ = Planning and Implementing Change

Profile Interpretation

Total Scores for Each of the Four Scales	Result	Indications
6 to 9	low	You do not usually cope well with changes associated with transitions in your life. You need assistance in learning more effective coping skills.
10 to 14	moderate	You are sometimes able to cope well with changes associated with transitions in your life. You can use additional assistance.
15 to 18	high	You most often cope successfully with changes associated with transitions in your life.

No matter how you scored, low, moderate or high, you will benefit from the exercises that follow.

Scale Descriptions

I. Perceiving and Responding to Transitions

This scale relates to your perceptions and responses to transitions in your life. The way you perceive your change is very important. People scoring high on this scale have a sense of self-control and self-esteem so that threatened changes are not perceived as overwhelming. These people are able to respond effectively to the initial shock or threat involved with a transition. They can describe the threat accurately, recognize the role of feelings in appraising the situation, and hold back impulsive or passive responses. This is indicative of their coping style.

II. Developing and Utilizing Internal/External Support Systems

This scale relates to your skills in assessing and using extra sources of emotional support during times of change. People who score high on this scale have the skills to identify their emotional needs, to identify people to be in their support network, and to reach out to them. People who score high in this category also use internal self-talk to provide critical and supportive messages during a transition. They can do this by becoming more aware of the irrational thoughts that lead to feelings of frustration and depression. In addition, they can visualize themselves as they would like to be.

III. Reducing Emotional and Physical Distress

This scale relates to your skills in managing the stressful effects associated with transitions. People scoring high on this scale are able to identify symptoms of distress and they respond effectively to stress. They can use a variety of methods for managing stress including meditation, rhythmic breathing, exercise, setting priorities, and thinking more realistically.

IV. Planning and Implementing Change

This scale relates to your skills in planning strategies for responding to transitions constructively. For people scoring high on this scale, planning the change is shown through the decisions they make during times of change. They may experience feelings of hesitation and anxiety about decisions, but they are able to use a rational approach to decision-making.

What is Your Coping Style?

Change is difficult for everyone. How do you cope with change? Place a check mark ☑ in each box that describes you.

1) I am an Optimist
- ❑ Very action-oriented
- ❑ Great at multitasking
- ❑ Not afraid to take risks
- ❑ Try to make change an opportunity for growth
- ❑ Want to move on quickly

2) I am an Idealist
- ❑ Very sensitive to the needs of others involved in the change
- ❑ Excellent team player who enjoys cooperative tasks and projects
- ❑ Peacemaker - seek harmony and inclusiveness
- ❑ Excellent interpersonal communicator
- ❑ Creative in interpersonal interactions

3) I am a Realist
- ❑ Very respectful of authority, rules, roles, and policies related to the change
- ❑ Very reliable and dependable a person who will complete tasks in an orderly fashion
- ❑ Understands priorities and sticks to them
- ❑ Practical, prepared, and efficient when approaching change
- ❑ Interested in seeing the immediate results regarding moving on from change

4) I am an Analyst
- ❑ Future-oriented and capable of visualizing the steps required to reach new goals
- ❑ Careful planner with a systematic approach to change
- ❑ Explore all facets of the problem before deciding on the best path to follow
- ❑ Persistent worker who will continue until problems with change are resolved
- ❑ Logical, analytical, and deductive problem-solver

Which style best describes you?

_____

_____

Which style clearly does not describe you?

_____

_____

Change Process

My latest change _____

The worst thing that can happen _____

_____.

I will lose _____

_____ because of this change.

I might gain _____

_____ because of this change.

This is affecting _____

_____.

My relationship with _____

_____.

I can plan _____

_____ to make the change smoother.

I need to decide _____

_____.

I can control _____

_____.

I cannot control _____

_____.

The possibilities for growth _____

_____.

Change Poetry

Write a poem about a change in your life.

For example:

My father passed away two months ago

I still miss him very much

I wish he were here to talk to me

I miss our conversations.

Think about how you feel or felt after going through a major change, and create a short poem to describe your feelings. Your poem does not have to rhyme.

_____

_____

_____

_____

_____

_____

_____

_____

_____

_____

_____

_____

_____

_____

_____

_____

_____

_____

_____

_____

_____

 © 2011 WHOLE PERSON ASSOCIATES, 101 WEST 2ND ST., SUITE 203, DULUTH MN 55802 ▪ 800-247-6789

What's The Worst That Could Happen?

Oftentimes we exaggerate the severity of changes we are going through by focusing on the negatives and thinking only about the worst things that could happen.

Describe a change you are currently going through or may soon experience:

_____

_____

_____

What are your feelings about the change?

_____

_____

_____

What is the very worst thing that you think could happen after the change?

_____

_____

_____

What are some of the more probable things that you think could happen?

_____

_____

_____

What actions can you take to make sure the worst does not happen?

_____

_____

_____

What actions can you take if the worst does happen?

_____

_____

_____

Positive Self Talk

Self-talk is the act of talking to yourself, either aloud or silently.
Positive self-talk takes place any time you think or talk to yourself
in a beneficial manner.

I'll try!	It's OK to ask for advice!
I just need to take the first step!	*This is NOT the end of the world!*
This just might work out well!	I accept the things I cannot control!
I can solve problems!	I will do my best!
It will bring out the best in me!	**Feeling reasonably anxious is OK!**
I've made changes before – I can do it again!	

Change Debate

Write your reasons, from both sides of the argument,
why change is bad or why change is good.

Change is a bad thing because ...

_____

_____

_____

_____

_____

_____

_____

_____

_____

_____

_____

Change is a good thing because ...

_____

_____

_____

_____

_____

_____

_____

_____

_____

_____

_____

_____

Newspaper Article
This will be a newspaper article about your change, happening now or in the past.

Headlines attract people to read the rest of a story. The headline stands out and is in a larger font than the story. The headline's message can be abrupt, and even startling. It describes quickly what the story covers. Its function is to attract attention. Begin with the headline and then tell your story.

#1 – Headline *(describe the change you experienced in 6 words or less)*:

_____

#2 – The change *(tell about your change)*

_____

_____

_____

#3 – Your feelings *(describe how you feel or felt)*

_____

_____

_____

#4 – Your life change *(describe how your life changed or is changing)*

_____

_____

_____

#5 – Coping *(describe how you coped or are coping with the changes)*

_____

_____

_____

My Change Management Skills

Managing change is a process.
Think about a change coming soon in your life.

What is the CHANGE?

_____

_____

_____

How will it AFFECT you?

_____

_____

_____

What might your decision be?

_____

_____

TIME TO DEVELOP A PLAN OF ACTION

What might your plan of action be for coping with this change?

Step 1. _____

_____

Step 2. _____

_____

Step 3. _____

_____

Step 4. _____

_____

My CHANGE Cartoon Strip

Everyone like cartoons! Cartoons can be very much like real life.

Example:

Think about a situation in the past when you had a huge change in your life.

Draw the change you experienced.

Now, draw how you coped and moved on.

Were there differences in the outcomes when you used different coping skills?

_____

_____

_____

_____

Why?

**When going through the stages of change, and trying
to manage them, it is important to remain true to your values.
Respond to the following WHY questions.**

The person I love very much is _____.

Why?_____.

The television program I like the most is _____.

Why?_____.

The person from history I admire most is _____.

Why?_____.

The work I value most is _____.

Why?_____.

The greatest job in the world would be _____.

Why?_____.

If I won a million dollars, I would spend it on _____.

Why?_____.

I am at my best when _____.

Why?_____.

The accomplishment I am most proud of is _____.

Why?_____.

For me, success is _____.

Why?_____.

(Continued on the next page)

Why? *(continued)*

The greatest job in my life _____.

Why?_____.

I do my best when _____.

Why?_____.

I daydream most about _____.

Why?_____.

What I want most in life is _____.

Why?_____.

My vision is _____.

Why?_____.

In my home, what I treasure the most is _____.

Why?_____.

My passion is _____.

Why?_____.

My proudest moment was _____.

Why?_____.

My family is _____.

Why?_____.

What did you learn about yourself and your values from this exercise?

_____

_____

_____

_____

Signature Strengths

Identify what you believe to be your greatest strengths.
Your strengths are important in managing change in your life. With a marker, highlight your best strengths in yellow. Then, in another color highlight your good strengths, and in a third color highlight your so-so strengths, ones that you can improve.

administering
analyzing
appraising
assembling
auditing
bargaining
budgeting
building
calculating
caring for others
communicating
computer work
conceptualizing
coordinating
copying
counseling
crafts
dancing
delegating
directing
drawing
driving
editing
empathizing
empowering
entertaining

estimating
executing orders
explaining
facilitating
filing
fixing cars
following instructions
gardening
getting things done
giving instructions
hair dressing
hypothesizing
influencing
installing
instructing
interviewing
inventing
keeping financial records
keeping records
knitting
listening
maintaining
making people laugh
making presentations
managing

mediating
mentoring
modeling
negotiating
nursing
nurturing
organizing
painting
performing
persuading
photography
planning
playing music
problem solving
projects
promoting
proofreading
protecting
providing guidance
publicizing
puzzles
questioning
raising money
rehabilitating
repairing

restoring
sandblasting
scrapbooking
selling
sewing
singing
sketching
solving statistical problems
speaking
supervising
synthesizing
teaching
training
translating
trouble-shooting
tutoring
using tools
waiting on others
weaving
working with machines
writing stories or books
writing proposals
writing speeches

Think - how can you use these strengths in your life during and after your change?

Doodling

Doodling is an excellent way for you to unleash the power of
self-expression. You do not need to be an artist to doodle.
You are the only one who needs to know what the doodle represents.
Doodling is simply drawing something without thinking a lot about it.
It is designed to help you put your logical left brain on hold
while you use your creative right brain.

My upcoming change…	*The reason I am anxious…*
I might gain…	*I will look like this after the change…*

Ways to Cope with Change

Table of Contents and Facilitator Notes

After the handouts are completed, ask for a volunteer to write on a board or flip chart. Participants can call out the ways they can slow down at work (items they wrote in the letter S [At Work]) and the volunteer will write them. Another volunteer can write the At Home responses, etc.

Before distributing the handouts, describe a change of the fictitious Mary James (moving to another city with a partner, 4 children, 2 cats, a hamster and a dog), and ask the group to first brainstorm what negative thoughts might be going through Mary's mind and then brainstorm the positive thoughts Mary might be developing. Then, distribute the handouts.

Examples of new projects might be learning a new language, upgrading computer skills, clean a closet, take an art class, volunteer at a soup kitchen, etc.

Ask if any of the participants are willing to share their responses on the second last sentence starter, "I can be outdoors and..."

You might want to distribute the handouts and then, before anyone begins, give an example of the Past Changes process.

Discuss with the group the functions and importance of supports. Then distribute handouts.

Table of Contents and Facilitator Notes

Ways to Cope with Change
Scale Introduction

One of the best ways to deal with change in your life is to learn how to cope effectively with it. People have varying levels of skills for coping with change, as well as preferred methods for coping.

This assessment is designed to help you understand how effectively you are in preventing and coping with change.

This scale will assess your skills for coping with change. Read each statement carefully. Circle the number of the response under the column **True**, **Somewhat True** or **Not True** to show how descriptive each statement is of you. Do NOT pay attention to the number itself, just the column. Please answer all the questions to the best of your ability.

In the following example, the circled 2 indicates that the statement is **Somewhat True** for the person completing the scale.

	True	Somewhat True	Not True
In dealing with change in my life…			
I am able to confront my mistaken beliefs	3	(2)	1

This is not a test and there are no right or wrong answers. Do not spend too much time thinking about your answers. Your initial response will be the most true for you. Be sure to respond to every statement.

Name _____ Date _____

Turn to the next page and begin.

Scale: Ways to Cope with Change

	True	Somewhat True	Not True
In dealing with change in my life…			
I am able to confront my mistaken beliefs	3	2	1
I find it difficult to stop and/or correct my self-talk.	1	2	3
I know how to monitor my negative self-talk	3	2	1
I sometimes question my worth as a human being	1	2	3
I can alter my expectations to match the changes occurring	3	2	1
I have many pessimistic thoughts	1	2	3
I often say things like "I can't change".	1	2	3
I can see the opportunities in a situation	3	2	1

I. TOTAL = _____

	True	Somewhat True	Not True
In dealing with change in my life…			
I often have a hard time coping	1	2	3
I exercise and keep physically fit	3	2	1
I manage my stress well	3	2	1
I waiver on the meaning and purpose in my life	1	2	3
I look to my religious and/or spiritual beliefs for comfort	3	2	1
I find it hard to get rest or enough sleep	1	2	3
I visualize reducing stress and anxiety.	3	2	1
I use relaxation techniques to relax my body	3	2	1

II. TOTAL = _____

Continued on the next page)

Scale: Ways to Cope with Change *(Continued)*

	True	Somewhat True	Not True
In dealing with change in my life…			
I have an adequate support system to help manage my stress . . .	3	2	1
I take care of myself and my personal needs.	3	2	1
I try to nurture myself when I feel anxious	3	2	1
I lose sight of my self-esteem	1	2	3
I am overly sensitive of critical statements from others	1	2	3
I do not try to live up to the expectations of others	3	2	1
I am not comfortable saying "no" in any situation	1	2	3
I am assertive in asking for what I want	3	2	1

III. TOTAL = _____

	True	Somewhat True	Not True
In dealing with change in my life…			
I often try to control the things I cannot control	1	2	3
I focus on the things in my life I can do something about	3	2	1
I am action oriented	3	2	1
I set new goals for myself and work toward them.	3	2	1
I make rational, logical decisions.	3	2	1
If one path does not work, I try another	3	2	1
I tend to give up easily	1	2	3
I let go of things beyond my control	3	2	1

IV. TOTAL = _____

GO TO THE SCORING DIRECTIONS

Ways to Cope with Change Scale Scoring Directions

Add the numbers you circled for each section on the scale and write that score on the line marked TOTAL at the end of the section.
Then transfer those totals to the spaces below.

I. Cognitive TOTAL   = _____   Your ability to alter your negative thinking, see change more realistically, and be more optimistic during times of change

II. Wellness TOTAL   = _____   Your ability to relax and manage stress during times of change

III. Nurturance TOTAL = _____   Your ability to take care of yourself during times of change

IV. Action TOTAL   = _____   Your ability to set goals, take positive action, and try to control only those things that you are able to control during times of change

Profile Interpretation

Individual Scales Scores	Result	Indications
19 to 24	high	If you score in the high range, you tend to be effective in coping with change in your life.
14 to 18	moderate	If you score in the moderate range, you have some skills in coping with change in your life.
8 to 13	low	If you score in the low range, you tend to have difficulty in coping with change in your life.

No matter how you scored, low, moderate or high, you will benefit from the exercises that follow.

© 2011 WHOLE PERSON ASSOCIATES, 101 WEST 2ND ST., SUITE 203, DULUTH MN 55802 • 800-247-6789

Slow Down!

Take some time to slow down. Realize that the thoughts and feelings you are experiencing are normal and are experienced by other people too. Whatever you are currently feeling, give yourself a break and try not to be so hard on yourself. Think about ways that you can slow your life down so that you can fully experience the change and provide time for you to process what has happened and plan for the future.

Write about the ways that you will slow down and relax a bit.

S At Work

_____

_____

_____

_____

_____

_____

_____

L At Home

_____

_____

_____

_____

_____

_____

_____

O With Friends

_____

_____

_____

_____

_____

_____

_____

W Others

_____

_____

_____

_____

_____

_____

_____

Your Thoughts

**Your thoughts greatly influence how effectively you are able to deal with the adversity that accompanies most changes.
Think about a recent change you have experienced or a change coming up.**

My change

_____

_____

_____

What negative thoughts go through your mind about this situation?

_____

_____

_____

_____

_____

_____

_____

What positive thoughts go through your mind about this situation?

_____

_____

_____

_____

_____

_____

_____

_____

Something New

**Sometimes beginning a new project will take your mind off of the changes you have been through or are going through.
Think about some new project you would like to engage in.**

What are some possible projects you might like to begin?

1. _____
2. _____
3. _____
4. _____
5. _____

Which one sounds best?

_____

Why did you choose this project?

_____
_____
_____
_____

What would you like to accomplish?

_____
_____
_____
_____

What do you need to do to make this happen?

_____
_____
_____
_____

I Can Cope By...

In the midst of a change of any kind, it is important to continue to think as positively as possible and to consider all of your resources. Respond to these sentence starters by writing the first thing that comes to your mind.

I can decide to _____

_____ as soon as possible.

I can call _____

_____.

I can go to _____

_____ for support.

I can help my body by _____

_____.

I can talk to _____

_____.

I can use my mind by _____

_____.

I can _____

_____ for my spirit.

I can improve my attitude by _____

_____.

I can be outdoors and _____

_____.

I can relax by _____

_____.

Past Changes

**Think about changes you experienced in the past.
How did you deal with major changes and transitions in the past?**

My biggest change in the last year was _____

_____

_____

_____

_____

_____

At first I _____

_____

_____

_____

_____

_____

After a while _____

_____

_____

_____

_____

_____

Now I _____

_____

_____

_____

_____

_____

Who Can Support You During Times of Change?

When you are experiencing change, it helps to talk with people who you trust. This system of people, your support system, can help you sort through your feeling, provide advice, make suggestions or just listen. Think about who can support you during times of change. List them below and why you feel they are good supports for you.

FAMILY MEMBERS

- Name _____

  Why? _____

- Name _____

  Why? _____

FRIENDS

- Name _____

  Why? _____

- Name _____

  Why? _____

SPIRITUAL / RELIGIOUS / COMMUNITY LEADER

- Name _____

  Why? _____

- Name _____

  Why? _____

OTHER ACQUAINTANCES

- Name _____

  Why? _____

- Name _____

  Why? _____

Take Time for Fun During Times of Change

**Fun activities can help to replenish your energy when it is waning.
They can lift up your spirit and rejuvenate you.
They are recreation/leisure-time experiences
in which you have fun and play.**

RATE THE FOLLOWING ACTIVITIES

1 *(doesn't sound like fun)* – **5** *(sounds like a blast!)*

___ Act	___ Genealogy	___ Religious groups
___ Bird watch	___ Handy work	___ Sculptor
___ Board Games	___ Health club	___ Silversmith
___ Book club	___ Hike	___ Sing
___ Cards	___ Investments	___ Social groups
___ Ceramics, clay, etc.	___ Journal	___ Spiritual groups
___ Choir	___ Knit, sew, crochet, etc.	___ Study group
___ Collections	___ Lapidary	___ Swim
___ Concert	___ Mah Jongg	___ Television
___ Cook or bake	___ Martial arts	___ Theater
___ Crafts	___ Metal work	___ Walk, run or jog
___ Cultural club	___ Movies	___ Watching indoor sports
___ Dance	___ Opera	___ Watching outdoor sports
___ Discussion group	___ Painting, drawing, etc.	___ Woodwork
___ Dog walk	___ Pets	___ Writing
___ Electronic games	___ Play an instrument	___ Yoga
___ Entertain	___ Playing an indoor sport	___ _____
___ Exercise	___ Playing an outdoor sport	___ _____
___ Fitness	___ Poetry	___ _____
___ Flower arranging	___ Political club	___ _____
___ Garden	___ Read	___ _____

Take a look at your 4's and 5's and have fun doing them!

Control or No Control

People who are able to adapt well to change take an active approach in dealing with it. They look for aspects of the change process they can control and they take action. They usually find that as they take action, they discover new possibilities and new supply of energy.

Describe a major change you have experienced or are currently experiencing:

_____

_____

_____

What were you able to control in the situation?

_____

_____

_____

What action did you take and what was the result?

_____

_____

_____

What were you not able to control in the situation?

_____

_____

_____

How were you able to accept the things you could not control?

_____

_____

_____

My Routines

People get into certain routines in their personal and professional lives. These routines provide us with comfort and familiarity. Change interrupts this comfort and familiarity.

Answer the following questions related to how a future change will affect your routine.

What is a change that will or might happen in your future?

_____

How would your routine be different because of the change?

_____

_____

_____

What would be the positive effects of the change on your routine?

_____

_____

_____

What would be the negative effects of the change on your routine?

_____

_____

_____

What would be your new routine?

_____

_____

_____

What new routines would you now like to create for yourself?

_____

_____

_____

Anything Goes!

When coping with changes in your life, it is important to take care of yourself through small acts of kindness toward yourself. Think about those things you could do on a daily basis to feel nurtured. Self-nurturing is important in your beginning to develop a loving relationship with yourself! In the spaces below, list the things that you could do to nurture yourself. Don't hold back. Remember that anything goes.

Realistic Ways I Would Like To Nurture Myself

_____	_____
_____	_____
_____	_____
_____	_____
_____	_____

Now prioritize by picking your top 5 and write how you can begin.

1. _____

   _____

   _____

2. _____

   _____

   _____

3. _____

   _____

   _____

4. _____

   _____

   _____

5. _____

   _____

   _____

Which of These Describe You Right Now?

- [ ] A glass half full
- [ ] A glass half empty
- [ ] A soaring airplane
- [ ] A burned out light bulb
- [ ] A sunny day
- [ ] A crying baby
- [ ] A deserted island
- [ ] A blossoming tree
- [ ] A blown out tire
- [ ] An octopus
- [ ] A mouse in a mouse trap
- [ ] The ocean at high tide

- [ ] An ice cream cone
- [ ] Swimming against the tide
- [ ] A car out of gas
- [ ] A flowering rose bush
- [ ] A cloudy day
- [ ] A colorful painting
- [ ] A motor boat
- [ ] Driving under the speed limit
- [ ] Driving over the speed limit
- [ ] A tree in the forest
- [ ] The last cookie in the cookie jar
- [ ] A piece of chocolate

Time to Energize

Exercise and movement activities are beneficial to keep you energized. Think of some of the activities you do that keep you energized. They do not need to be difficult or take a lot of time.

What are some of the things you do now that energize you?

_____   _____
_____   _____
_____   _____
_____   _____

What are some of the things you could start doing now that might energize you?

_____   _____
_____   _____
_____   _____
_____   _____

Fill in this chart each day for a week. As you do each activity, place a check mark.

Day	Time	Place	Activity	Done
Sunday				
Monday				
Tuesday				
Wednesday				
Thursday				
Friday				
Saturday				

© 2011 WHOLE PERSON ASSOCIATES, 101 WEST 2ND ST., SUITE 203, DULUTH MN 55802 ▪ 800-247-6789

Healthy Living

**Maintaining good health and wellness is important
in helping to combat the effects of unhealthy changes in your life.
Following are some wellness suggestions:**

Healthy Eating

Avoid: Caffeine, Alcohol, Salt, Red Meat, Nicotine, Chocolate, Sugar, Soda
Eat & Drink: Fruits, Whole-grain breads and cereals, Fresh vegetables, Nuts, Brown rice, Water, Fiber, Fish / Seafood

Quality Sleep

Get a good night's sleep
The bedroom is for sex and sleep, no TV or reading
Take "power" naps when you are able, but not too long and not to close to bedtime

Exercise and Fitness

Walk, jog or hike often
Participate in games or physical activities around the house
Engage in aerobic exercise for at least thirty minutes a day, three or four times per week

Recharge Your Batteries

Spend time with a significant other, with family or special friends
Develop personal and professional goals to attain
Continue to engage in your favorite leisure activities

Laugh

Watch funny movies, television shows, go to the theater, concerts, etc.
Be with people who are fun and laugh a lot
Read jokes, funny calendars and clever emails

Relax

Meditate
Breathe deep and do relaxation exercises
Take yoga, Pilates, etc.

Sexual Health

Healthy relationships
Safe sex
Planned pregnancies

Healthy Weight

Keep a healthy weight range for your age and height
Healthy nutritional regime
Exercise

Hope

It is important to have things to look forward to. Hope is the belief that your life will continue going well or will get better. It is important to develop a plan of activities that you can look forward to.

H – Have a list of what you will look forward to in the next week.

_____

_____

_____

_____

_____

O – Opt to have a wish-list of things to happen or accomplish in the next month.

_____

_____

_____

_____

_____

P – Plan for what you'd like to have happening in your life in a year.

_____

_____

_____

_____

_____

E – Everything and everyone you would like to have in your life in 5 years.

_____

_____

_____

_____

_____

My Attitude About Change

Table of Contents and Facilitator Notes

Prior to distributing handouts, discuss the premise that everyone makes mistakes, and especially when facing a life change. It might be a change in attitude, resistance, or reactions. By acknowledging our mistakes we are able to do better next time.

If you think it will be helpful, brainstorm with the group a scenario of a change and the actions listed on the Choosing Action handout prior to distributing handouts.

After the handouts have been completed, ask participants if they had other strategies they added to the list on the top half of the page. List them on a board.

After handouts are completed, ask participants who wish to share their caricatures.

Provide color pencils, markers and/or crayons for participants to write their responses and/or to decorate the container.

Possible examples to share with the participants:
    CHANGE: Lost my job.
        family life: *I didn't have to put in so much overtime.*
        personal life: *I never liked the job, therefore I was happier.*
        professional life: *Even though it took a while, I found a job I liked better.*
        family life: *When mama's happy, everyone's happy!*
        health and wellness: *I wasn't working such long hours and now have time to exercise.*
        financial life: *I make the same money but it's not so far to drive. Less gasoline!*

Distribute handouts and discuss the meaning of motivation prior to group working on handout. Provide highlighters if available.

Table of Contents and Facilitator Notes

My Attitude About Change
Scale Introduction

To deal with change in the future, work on developing effective coping attitudes and skills. These attitudes and skills include thinking about change in new ways, setting constructive goals, finding meaning and purpose, and developing effective problem-solving strategies.

The *My Attitude About Change Scale* can help you identify and explore your current attitudes and skills related to dealing with change in your life.

The assessment contains 22 statements. With YES or NO as your choice, read each of the statements and circle the word which best describes whether the statement applies to you or not.

	YES	NO
When it comes to change in my life...		
I feel it is not a normal part of life 2		(1)

In the above statement, the circled number under NO means that the statement is not like the participant.

This is not a test and there are no right or wrong answers. Do not spend too much time thinking about your answers. Your initial response will be the most true for you. Be sure to respond to every statement.

Name _____ **Date** _____

Turn to the next page and begin.

Scale: My Attitudes About Change

	YES	NO

When it comes to change in my life…

	YES	NO
I feel it is not a normal part of life	2	1
I believe it is not a good thing	1	2
I blame others for what is happening	1	2
I view change as a hurdle to jump to get where I want to go	2	1
I am not a worrier	2	1
I rarely feel powerless	2	1
I enjoy a good challenge	2	1
I get anxious and depressed	1	2
I refuse to let change disrupt my life	2	1
I tend to think the worst, first	1	2
I do not panic when I encounter change	2	1
My self-talk says, "Why me?"	1	2
I have supportive people in my life who help me	2	1
I can control it	2	1
Life is not fair	1	2
I feel like there is no good solution	1	2
I get scared	1	2
I envision ways I can grow from it	2	1
I see it as a challenge	2	1
I feel unlucky	1	2
I manage the stress associated with it	2	1
I think that this happens to me only	1	2

TOTAL = _____

GO TO THE SCORING DIRECTIONS

My Attitude About Change Scale
Scoring Directions

The onset of change requires specific skills and attitudes to work efficiently through a change in a positive manner. The *My Attitude About Change Scale* is designed to measure the proficiency of your skills and attitudes for coping with change in your life and to provide activities to enhance your skills and attitudes for coping.

For each of the items you completed, add the number that you circled for each item. Put that total on the line marked TOTAL at the end of the section.

Then, transfer your total to the space below:

My Attitude about Change TOTAL = _____

Profile Interpretation

Individual Scale Scores	Result	Indications
0 to 7	low	If you scored in the low range on the scale, you lack sufficient attitudes and skills to cope effectively with change.
8 to 14	moderate	If you scored in the moderate range on the scale, you have sufficient attitudes and skills to cope effectively with change, but you can improve.
15 to 22	high	If you scored in the high range on the scale, you definitely have the attitudes and skills to cope effectively with change.

No matter how you scored, low, moderate or high, you will benefit from the exercises that follow.

Learn From Your Mistakes

Mistakes can provide you with insight on how to deal with change more effectively. Reflect upon some of the changes in your life.

CHANGE IN MY LIFE	MISTAKES IN HOW I HANDLED THE CHANGE	WHAT I'VE LEARNED

Choosing Action

To effectively deal with change, you will need to develop a plan.

My current or future change is…	
First, I need to…	
Next, I will…	
I can minimize my stress by…	
Who else is involved? I can help minimize their stress by…	
Who can help me plan?	
I want the result(s) to be…	
I am able to control…	
I can ensure a positive result by…	

Coping Strategies

**Going through the stage of change
can stir up a variety of emotions, many of which can be negative.
How can you continue to focus on the positive aspects of the change?
Check off coping strategies that you are willing to try.**

My Change _____

I will...

___	remain positive when talking about it	___	meditate and engage in other relaxation techniques
___	reach out to a supportive person	___	express myself
___	be proud of small steps	___	use positive self-talk
___	give myself a reward for each step	___	talk to someone who listens well
___	not say "This will never work"	___	seek spiritual support
___	forget about other unsuccessful changes	___	keep my sense of humor
___	take deep breaths	___	_____
___	keep inspiring quotes nearby	___	_____
___	not minimize the change	___	_____
___	remember I don't need to be perfect	___	_____
___	take care of my body	___	_____
___	not exaggerate issues		

List three of the coping skills above that you are willing to focus on and describe examples of how you might channel your energies.

1. _____

_____

_____

2. _____

_____

_____

3. _____

_____

_____

Caricatures

**Caricatures are exaggerated or distorted likenesses.
You don't need to be an artist to draw caricatures. They just need to make
sense to you as to what change looks like in your mind.**

EXAMPLE: Time to retire and I'm worried about having enough money.

Draw a caricature of one of the changes in your life.

My Future Container

This container is specifically designed to hold your future. In it you can put anything you would like to indicate what you hope for your future. What will you put into your box and how will that object remind you of changes in your future. You can write your hopes on the lines. You can decorate the box when you're finished.

© 2011 WHOLE PERSON ASSOCIATES, 101 WEST 2ND ST., SUITE 203, DULUTH MN 55802 ▪ 800-247-6789

My Positive Changes

List a time in your life when something positive came out of
a change in any of the following aspects of your life.

The Change _____

Positive changes in my family life:

_____

_____

_____

Positive changes in my personal life:

_____

_____

_____

Positive changes in my professional life:

_____

_____

_____

Positive changes in my social life:

_____

_____

_____

Positive changes in my health & wellness:

_____

_____

_____

Positive changes in my financial life:

_____

_____

_____

Positive changes in my spiritual / religious life:

_____

_____

_____

What Motivates You?

Definition of MOTIVE:

motive \ 'mō-tiv: a need or desire that causes a person to take action

List a recent or upcoming change _____

_____

What will motivate you to cope with this change?

HIGHLIGHT OR PUT A CHECK MARK AFTER YOUR MOTIVATIONS.

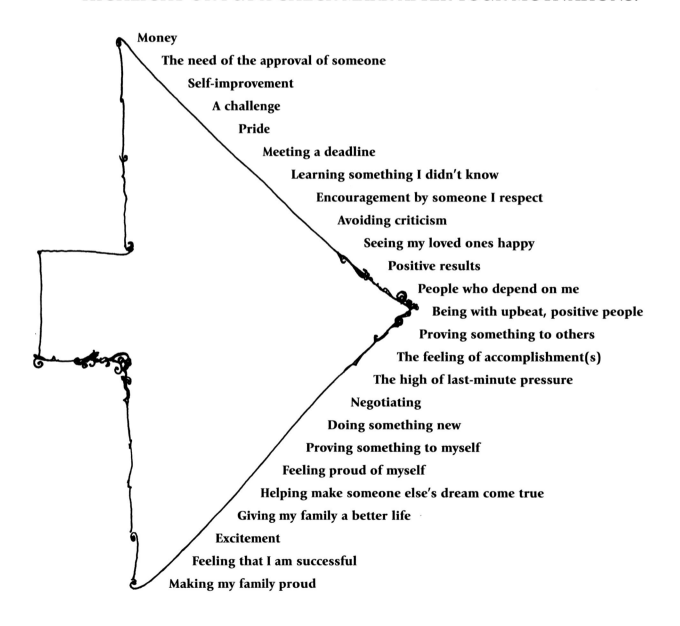

Money

The need of the approval of someone

Self-improvement

A challenge

Pride

Meeting a deadline

Learning something I didn't know

Encouragement by someone I respect

Avoiding criticism

Seeing my loved ones happy

Positive results

People who depend on me

Being with upbeat, positive people

Proving something to others

The feeling of accomplishment(s)

The high of last-minute pressure

Negotiating

Doing something new

Proving something to myself

Feeling proud of myself

Helping make someone else's dream come true

Giving my family a better life

Excitement

Feeling that I am successful

Making my family proud

List Making

Making lists can be very effective in helping you organize and manage your changes.

List the things you would do all over again if you could live your life over.

List the changes you would like to make in your life.

My Role Model

We all have people who inspire us in different ways.
A helpful strategy is to think of someone you admire who made a change
in his/her life or the life of others and managed the change well.

Your role model: _____

What change did your role-model experience?

_____
_____
_____
_____
_____
_____

How did that person manage their change?

_____
_____
_____
_____
_____
_____

What words of encouragement do you think that person might give to you?

_____
_____
_____
_____
_____
_____

Renewed Purpose and Meaning

Sometimes, change creates a feeling of loss of purpose and meaning. Your purpose and meaning must be recognized and renewed in order for you to move on more easily after a change in life. Purpose can come from past passions and from the creation of new passions based on the life experiences you are having.

What passions did you have in the past that you might like to renew?

_____

_____

_____

_____

What new interests, that could grow into passions, might you be interested in developing?

_____

_____

_____

_____

What obstacles could keep you from pursuing these passions?

_____

_____

_____

_____

How can you overcome these obstacles?

_____

_____

_____

_____

_____

_____

Reframing Negative Beliefs

Some beliefs that could hold you back from achieving success in most of your life changes:

A *"These kinds of things happen only to me"* ____

B *"I'm a failure"* ____

C *"I can't win"* ____

D *"It was the only thing that made me happy"* ____

E *"Life is unfair"* ____

F *"I can't do anything else"* ____

G *"If I ignore it, it will not happen"* ____

H *"If I wait long enough, the situation will change"* ____

I *"This is the worst thing that can happen to me"* ____

J *"I am the most unlucky person alive"* ____

Reframing the thoughts above will help you change your attitude to a positive one.

Find the statement below that reframes one of the statements above and put the number that is on the left next to the negative statement above.

1 *"Maybe I wasn't so successful this time, but I have been before and will again"*

2 *"I'm going to find other things to do that I do well"*

3 *"I have other things that make me happy"*

4 *"I am fortunate in many ways"*

5 *"Everyone experiences some kind of change"*

6 *"I need to be proactive"*

7 *"I'm not going to put my head in the sand and hide"*

8 *"I win some and lose some, like most people"*

9 *"Things could be so much worse"*

10 *"Life might not always be fair, but I have a lot to be grateful for"*

And I Grew

**After successfully coping with changes in your life, a new you
will emerge and you will grow from the experience.
Describe a change you went through in your life.**

_____

_____

On the lines below, using one word only, list the positive things that came out of that change for you and how you grew.

How Proactive Are You?

There are steps you can take to be proactive in getting what you want after transitions in life. Write about an upcoming change that you know is about to happen.

What is the change?

_____

_____

Was this your choice?

_____

_____

How do you feel about it?

_____

_____

_____

What would you like to get out of your new situation?

_____

_____

_____

_____

How will you be proactive to make it happen?

_____

_____

_____

_____

How do you think you will grow from this change?

_____

_____

_____

_____

My New Attitude Shining Through

Dealing with change can make you feel overwhelmed, and you might begin to develop a negative attitude. Remember that just as you have developed negative attitudes, you can just as easily develop positive attitudes. You can begin to develop a new attitude by focusing on the positive aspects in your life. Sometimes these positive aspects of your life are hidden behind dark clouds, and it is time to let your new attitude shine through. The following sentence starters will help you to focus on the positives in your life.

I am generous …

_____

_____

I am thankful for…

_____

_____

I am unique …

_____

_____

My family is …

_____

_____

I am attractive …

_____

_____

I love myself for …

_____

_____

Ways I am healthy …

_____

_____

I celebrate myself by…

_____

_____

I dream of …

_____

_____

I have friends who…

_____

_____

My Goals

To begin moving on from change, it helps to have a positive attitude and to work toward your future. Goal setting is a way to maintain a positive attitude and move you in a positive direction. Try it for yourself.

The change that occurred in my life: _____

_____

_____

_____

_____

MY GOALS IN BUILDING A POSITIVE NEW FUTURE

In the **next week** I will _____

_____

_____

_____

_____

In the **next month** I will _____

_____

_____

_____

_____

Within the **year** I will _____

_____

_____

_____

_____

Signed _____   Date _____

Whole Person Associates is the leading publisher of training resources for professionals who empower people to create and maintain healthy lifestyles. Our creative resources will help you work effectively with your clients in the areas of stress management, wellness promotion, mental health and life skills.

Please visit us at our web site: **WholePerson.com**. You can check out our entire line of products, place an order, request our print catalog, and sign up for our monthly special notifications.

Whole Person Associates

800-247-6789